DATE DUE

IRAN
the culture

Joanne Richter

A Bobbie Kalman Book

The Lands, Peoples, and Cultures Series

Crabtree Publishing Company
www.crabtreebooks.com

The Lands, Peoples, and Cultures Series

Created by Bobbie Kalman

Coordinating editor
Ellen Rodger

Project editor
Rachel Eagen

Production coordinator
Rosie Gowsell

Project development, design, editing, and photo editing
First Folio Resource Group, Inc.
  Tom Dart
  Greg Duhaney
  Debbie Smith

Research
April Fast

Proofreading
Carolyn Black

Photo research
Maria DeCambra

Consultants
Dr. Mehrangiz Nikou, Massoume Price

Photographs
Abbas/Magnum Photos: p. 24, p. 25, p. 27; AP Photo/Kamran Jebreili: p. 20 (right); AP Photo/Enric Marti: p. 17 (left); AP Photo/Vahid Salemi: title page, p. 12, p. 15 (right); AP Photo/Hasan Sarbakhshian: p. 13, p. 16, p. 20 (left), p. 21 (both); AP Photo/Afshin Valinejad: p. 11 (right); Archivo Iconografico, S.A./Corbis: p. 8 (left); Art Archive/Archaeological Museum Teheran/Dagli Orti: p. 22 (left); Art Archive/Dagli Orti: p. 26 (bottom); Art Directors/Michael Good: p. 8 (right), p. 17 (right); Maher Attar/Corbis Sygma: p. 9 (right); Dave Bartruff/Corbis: p. 18 (right); Bildarchiv Preussischer Kulturbesitz/Art Resource, NY: p. 4 (top); Bridgeman-Giraudon/Art Resource, NY: p. 28; Corbis: p. 23 (left); Rad Eslami/Gamma/Ponopresse: p. 11 (left), p. 14 (right); Atta Kenare/AFP/Getty Images: p. 10, p. 18 (left); Earl & Nazima Kowall/Corbis: p. 9 (left); Peter Langer - Associated Media Group: cover; Chris Lisle/Corbis: p. 26 (top); Behrouz Mehri/AFP/Getty Images: p. 14 (left), p. 15 (left); Nadji/Paris Match - Gamma/Ponopresse: p. 29 (right); Michael Nicholson/Corbis: p. 3; Diego Lezama Orezzoli/Corbis: p. 6 (left); Claudio Papi/Reuters/Corbis: p. 5 (bottom); The Pierpont Morgan Library/ Art Resource, NY: p. 23 (right); Reuters/Corbis: p. 19 (top), p. 29 (left); SEF/Art Resource, NY: p. 19 (bottom); Stapleton Collection/ Corbis: p. 22 (right); Ramin Talaie/Corbis: p. 6 (right); David Turnley/Corbis: p. 5 (top), p. 7; Roger Wood/Corbis: p. 4 (bottom)

Illustrations
Dianne Eastman: icon
David Wysotski, Allure Illustrations: back cover
Blair Drawson: pp. 30–31

Cover: The Azadi Square Monument, built in 1971, is the gateway to Iran's capital city, Tehran.

Title page: On Women's Day, Iranian women fight for equal rights and freedoms. These women, who are performing in a show, are dressed according to the Muslim custom of *hijab*, a dress code that requires women to be covered from head to toe to protect their modesty. *Hijab* is mandatory in Iran.

Icon: A *samovar*, or urn in which hot water is boiled for tea, appears at the head of each section. At first, *samovars* in Iran were used only by the wealthy, but now they are common in everyone's homes.

Back cover: The *gandar*, or Iranian crocodile, grows to be ten to thirteen feet (three to four meters) long. In winter, it floats in rivers or basks in the sun. In summer, it lies in mud that forms at the bottom of rivers that dry out in the heat.

Crabtree Publishing Company

www.crabtreebooks.com   1-800-387-7650

Cataloging-in-Publication-Data
Richter, Joanne.
  Iran, the culture / Joanne Richter.
    p. cm. -- (Lands, peoples, and cultures)
  Includes index.
  ISBN-13: 978-0-7787-9317-5 (rlb)
  ISBN-10: 0-7787-9317-6 (rlb)
  ISBN-13: 978-0-7787-9685-5 (pbk)
  ISBN-10: 0-7787-9685-X (pbk)
  1. Iran--Civilization--Juvenile literature. 2. Iran--Social life and customs--Juvenile literature. I. Title. II. Lands, peoples, and cultures series
  DS266.R53 2005
  955--dc22
                    2005001078
                         LC

Published in the United States
PMB 16A
350 Fifth Ave.
Suite 3308
New York, NY
10118

Published in Canada
616 Welland Ave.
St. Catharines
Ontario, Canada
L2M 5V6

Published in the United Kingdom
73 Lime Walk
Headington
Oxford
0X3 7AD
United Kingdom

Published in Australia
386 Mt. Alexander Rd.
Ascot Vale (Melbourne)
V1C 3032

Contents

Crossroads of culture

In the cool early night, after prayer, Iranians gather at an open-air teahouse to relax with friends. A traditional covered market twists its way through the heart of the city. Its brightly lit shops are filled with patterned carpets, brass and wooden crafts, vegetables, grains, and spices. In a nearby home, a mother cleans up after a dinner of soup, yogurt, and fresh, warm bread, while her children study their Persian grammar before bed. Welcome to Iran.

Part of the Persian Empire

Iran lies in the region known as the Middle East, which borders the southern and eastern shores of the Mediterranean Sea. For thousands of years, the country was known to outsiders as Persia, after a province in the southwest that was once called Parsa. The people within the country called their land Iran, meaning "country of the Aryan peoples," for the Aryan peoples who moved to Iran from central Asia. These settlers included the Persians, who came to the region beginning around 1300 B.C.

(top) Iran is known for its beautiful, handwoven carpets, which are made of wool and silk. The designs of many carpets are inspired by the designs on tiles and by small, detailed paintings, called miniatures, created long ago.

By 558 B.C., the Persian people controlled a large region in the Middle East, including Iran and the neighboring lands. Today, Iran's art, music, food, literature, and languages all have roots in the first Persian **Empire**. Iran's culture has also been influenced by the many other peoples who invaded and conquered Iran over time.

(above) Muslim men bow and kneel as they pray at a mosque, or place of worship, in the capital city of Tehran. They remove their shoes and wash their faces, hands, and feet before entering the mosque because cleanliness while praying is considered a sign of respect for God.

The Islamic Revolution

In 1979, a revolution known as the Islamic Revolution took place in Iran. It deeply affected the country's culture. Iran became an Islamic **republic**, a country whose rules follow the laws of Islam. Islam is a religion that teaches that there is one God, whom **Muslims** call Allah, and that Muhammad was his final **prophet**.

The first ruler of the Islamic republic was a religious leader named Ayatollah Ruhollah Khomeini. Khomeini outlawed all forms of culture that he felt went against the teachings of Islam. Since Khomeini's death in 1989, different forms of expression that were once banned are now allowed. Today, Iranian craftspeople, painters, musicians, and writers explore new themes in their work while respecting the old traditions. Iranian directors and actors portray life in Iran in films that appeal to audiences around the world.

The Magnificent Victory of the Islamic Revolution of Iran is celebrated every February 22 to mark the day that Ayatollah Khomeini rose to power in 1979.

Abbas Khiarostami, shown on the right, is an award-winning filmmaker whose movies are known for their poetic language and political and philosophical messages. His films include The Wind Will Carry Us, *starring actor Behzad Dourani, shown on the left, about the mysterious visit of four city-dwellers to a remote village.*

Islam

In 610 A.D., in the land known today as Saudi Arabia, a man named Muhammad heard the angel Jibril whispering in his ear. Jibril told Muhammad that he had been chosen to share the teachings of God, whose name in Arabic is Allah, with fellow Arabians. A new religion, Islam, developed around Muhammad's leadership.

Islam came to Iran in 651 A.D., when Arabian armies migrated from their land to spread Muhammad's message after his death. Today, about 98 percent of Iran's people are Muslims.

(top) The Sheikh Lotfollah Mosque, in the central city of Isfahan, was built between 1602 and 1619. The king, Shah Abbas I, used it as a royal mosque. Its entranceway is decorated with beautiful blue and yellow mosaic tiles.

Islam's holy books

Muhammad received Allah's words in the form of verses that Jibril taught him. Scribes wrote down the verses that Muhammad recited, and hundreds of Muhammad's followers memorized them. The collection of these written verses is known as the *Qur'an*. The *Qur'an* is the most important Muslim holy book. Its 114 chapters, written in Arabic, outline Islam's laws governing prayer, family, **trade**, and the punishment of crimes. Muslims also follow a second holy book, the *Hadith*, which is a collection of Muhammad's words and deeds as recorded by his followers.

(above) Friday is the holiest day of the Muslim week. It represents the sixth day of creation, on which Allah completed his work. Muslims gather to say special midday prayers on Friday. Offices, banks, and post offices are closed, but in large cities such as Tehran, stores remain open.

Muslim men and women are not allowed to pray together. Devout, or deeply religious, women often pray in separate sections of mosques, or they pray at home or work.

Shi'is and Sunnis

When Muhammad died, his followers formed into groups according to their beliefs about how future religious leaders should be chosen. One group, who became known as the Shi'is, believed that Muhammad had expected his cousin and son-in-law, Ali, to lead in his place. They felt that only Ali's **descendants** could be the rightful leaders of Islam. These leaders are known as *imams*. Another group, the Sunnis, believed that future leaders should be elected from among Muhammad's followers. Over the years, other differences developed between Shi'is and Sunnis, including the fact that each group has its own version of the *Hadith*.

About 90 percent of Iranians belong to the Jafari, or Twelver, Shi'i branch of Islam. Jafari Shi'is believe that the twelfth *imam*, known as Imam Mahdi or Imam Zaman, disappeared in the 800s, but never died. They believe that he will return one day to lead his people. Jafari Shi'i Islam has been Iran's official religion since 1501.

Shi'i principles of faith

The Shi'i faith in Iran is based on five *usul al-din*, or principles.

1. *Tawhid*, or one God: Muslims accept that there is no God but Allah.

2. *Nabovat*, or prophethood: Muslims accept that Allah has chosen prophets to bring his message to the world, and that Muhammad was the final prophet.

3. *Maad*, or resurrection: Muslims accept that a day of resurrection will occur. On this day, Allah will bring the dead back to life, judge them for their actions while they were alive, and then send them to either **Heaven** or **Hell**.

4. *Adl*, or divine justice: Muslims accept that Allah is fair.

5. *Imamat*, or imamate: Shi'i Muslims believe that Allah, not the people, selects the leaders of Islam.

Sufism

The prophet Muhammad is said to have told Muslims to understand Islam through his words, his deeds, and his inspiration. Muslims who practice Sufism believe that there is a mysterious aspect of Islam that they can know only by freeing their minds of everyday cares and focusing on Allah. They believe that music, poetry, and dance help connect them to Allah. Sufism was once very popular and accepted in Iran, but today, Iranian Sufis face discrimination, because Muslim leaders feel that their practices stray too far from the basic teachings of Islam.

A mihrab, such as this one in Isfahan's Friday Mosque, or Masjid-e Jom'eh, is a small alcove that shows the direction of Mecca. Muslims must face in the direction of this holy city as they pray.

Duties of Islam

Shi'is show their devotion to Allah by carrying out a number of *furu al-din*, or duties. These include *namaz*, or prayer to Allah, three times a day, and *roozeh*, which means fasting. Muslims must fast, or go without food and water, between dawn and dusk throughout the holy month of *Ramazan*. "Ramazan" is known in Arabic as "Ramadan." Another duty is *hajj*, or pilgrimage. At least once in their lifetimes, Muslims who are healthy and financially able must travel to the holy city of Mecca, in present-day Saudi Arabia. Mecca is the birthplace of Muhammad and the site of the most important Muslim **shrine**.

An official called a muezzin calls Muslims to prayer from a minaret, or tower, high atop a mosque. The call, a haunting chant that praises Allah, is delivered either in person or from a tape recording, and is transmitted by loudspeaker to the surrounding community.

Sufis, known as dervishes, enter trance-like states by repeatedly reciting chants that praise Allah. Some people consider dervishes holy, believing that they can perform miracles and predict the future.

Iran also has female religious leaders, who study at separate religious schools. There, they learn how to lead all-women's prayer services, as Muslim men and women are not allowed to pray together. Female religious leaders are not promoted through a series of ranks as men are.

Shari'ah

Shari'ah is a system of law that guides Muslim life. It is based on the writings of the *Qur'an* and the *Hadith*. *Shari'ah* covers topics, such as how to pray and fast, and it outlines rules for trade and marriage. *Shari'ah* also tells Muslims how to behave in public and private in order to please Allah. The Islamic Republic of Iran is run according to the laws of *Shari'ah*, as interpreted by the religious leaders there.

Religious leaders

Iran has many traditional Muslim colleges, called *madrasahs*, where men study Muslim law and join the *ulama*, or group of religious leaders. Most members of the Shi'i *ulama*, who are known as *mullahs*, leave the *madrasah* to work as prayer leaders or to run mosques. A few *mullahs* are promoted through a series of ranks over their lifetimes.

One high rank is that of a *mujtahid*, a religious leader who is allowed to **interpret** Muslim law. *Mujtahids* have studied at *madrasahs* for at least fifteen years, have won the respect of other *mujtahids*, and have gained followers among fellow students. As *mujtahids* grow more knowledgeable through their studies and gain more followers through preaching and writing, they may eventually be named *ayatollahs* or even grand *ayatollahs* by a council of elders. *Ayatollah* means "sign of God," and is one of the highest ranks of religious leadership.

Mullahs in Iran wear white turbans and loose, sleeveless brown or black cloaks called abbas. Those who descend directly from Muhammad wear black turbans, and are given special respect. These mullahs study at the madrasah in the northcentral city of Qom, one of the largest madrasahs in Iran.

 # Other faiths

Iran recognizes Zoroastrianism, Judaism, and Christianity as religious minorities. People of these faiths are officially free to follow their traditions and receive a religious education. Since the 1979 Islamic Revolution, however, the government allows only Muslims to run the private schools of these minorities, and it must approve any religious texts written in Persian. In order to attend university, people of religious minorities must pass an exam on Islam, and some non-Muslims have been arrested for supposedly working against Islam.

Zoroastrianism

Thousands of years ago, an Iranian prophet named Zoroaster preached of one all-powerful god, called Ahura Mazda. Fire, believed to be one of Ahura Mazda's creations, became a symbol of the god, and Zoroastrian temples were built around constantly burning fire pits.

Today, about 20,000 Zoroastrians live in Iran, mostly in the capital city of Tehran and in the central city of Yazd. Among their traditions is a special ceremony that welcomes children between the ages of seven and fifteen to the religion. At the ceremony, a child puts on a shirt called a *sedra*, and the priest ties a *kusti*, or sacred cord, around his or her waist. The *sedra* and *kusti* were once worn beneath clothes every day for the rest of a Zoroastrian's life. Today, traditional Zoroastrians wear *sedras* and *kustis* when they get married or during special celebrations.

(top) Every year, Zoroastrians take part in a five-day pilgrimage to the ancient Chakchak temple, in central Iran. They hope to purify themselves and have their prayers answered at the temple.

Christianity

Around 300,000 Christians live in Iran today. Christians believe that Jesus Christ is the **savior** of the world, and that his father is God. Most Christians in Iran have **ancestors** from Armenia, a country north of Iran, or Assyria, an ancient land that once stood to the west. They live in cities such as Tehran, Urmia, Tabriz, and Isfahan.

Every December 1, Iranian Christians begin a fast. They eat no meat, eggs, milk, or cheese until Christmas Day, December 25. On Christmas Day, they celebrate Jesus Christ's birth by feasting on a traditional chicken stew called *harissa*, or on roast turkey. Iranian children celebrating Christmas receive new clothes, but rarely other gifts.

Judaism

Between 25,000 and 30,000 Jewish people live in Iran. They make up the largest Jewish community in the Middle East, outside of Israel. Many Jews fled Iran after the Islamic Revolution, moving to North America or to Israel. Jews believe in one God and study his teachings, which are recorded in their holy book, the *Torah*. Among the Jewish holidays are *Rosh Hashanah*, the Jewish New Year; *Yom Kippur*, the Day of **Atonement**; and *Pesach*, or Passover, which celebrates the freeing of the Jews from slavery thousands of years ago.

An Iranian Jew prays in front of a **menorah**, *a seven-branched candlestick that is a symbol of Judaism.*

The Armenian Church and Monastery of St. Thaddeus, known in Iran as the Kara Kelisa, or Black Church, is the site of an annual pilgrimage by Armenian Christians. According to Armenian legend, St. Thaddeus, one of Jesus Christ's disciples, or followers, built the world's first church at this northwestern site around 66 A.D.

The Baha'i faith

In 1844, a Shi'i Muslim from Shiraz, Sayyid Ali Muhammad, announced the coming of a new prophet. Sayyid Ali Muhammad's many followers called him the Bab, which means "gateway" in Arabic, since he believed that his role was to prepare people for the new prophet. Muslim leaders considered the Bab a false leader, since Islam states that Muhammad was Allah's final prophet. The Bab was arrested and killed, as were many of his followers.

In 1863, one of the Bab's greatest followers, an Iranian named Mizra Husayn-Ali, announced that he was the great prophet the Bab had spoken of. He became known as Baha'u'llah, or "Glory of God," and his followers became known as Baha'is. The Baha'i faith is based on Baha'u'llah's message that all people belong to a single family and should work together toward world peace. Around 300,000 Baha'is live in Iran today, but some of them hide their faith, since Baha'is are not allowed to attend university or work in the government, and can seldom own property.

Observing religious holidays

The most meaningful religious holiday of the year for Iranian Muslims is *Ramazan*. *Ramazan* remembers the time when the angel Jibril first whispered Allah's words to Muhammad. During this month of fasting and prayer, observant Muslims do not eat or drink between sunrise and sunset. This teaches them self-discipline and compassion for those who do not have enough food to eat.

Muslims awaken before dawn to eat a meal called *sahari.* This meal usually includes bread, cheese, tea, eggs, and dates. They break the fast after sunset, usually beginning with a single date and a prayer of thanks, and ending with a hearty feast called *iftari. Iftari* often features a traditional soup or stew.

The Night of *Qadr*

The *Hadith* tells Muslims that the last ten days of *Ramazan* are the holiest days of the holiest month of the year. The Night of *Qadr*, when Muhammad received the words of Allah from Jibril, falls during this time. Devoted Muslims say extra prayers on these days, and some even spend all ten days and nights at a mosque.

(top) **A muezzin's** *call awakens Iranians each morning during* **Ramazan,** *giving them time to eat before the fast and prayers begin.*

Thousands of Iranians gather for prayers to mark the beginning of Eid-e Fetr.

Eid-e Fetr

Ramazan ends with the joyous festival of *Eid-e Fetr*. Devout Iranians celebrate this day by attending religious services and sharing a feast with family and friends. They greet each other with, *"Eid Mubarak!"*, which means "Have a blessed *Eid*." The festivities last for one day in Iran.

Eid-e Qurban

Eid-e Qurban, or the Feast of the Sacrifice, recalls the story of the prophet Ibrahim, who lived thousands of years ago. In a series of dreams, Ibrahim received a message that he must kill his only son, Ismail, to please Allah. Wanting to make Allah happy, Ibrahim went to the **altar** with Ismail and drew his sword. Before Ibrahim could kill Ismail, Allah stopped him and told him to **sacrifice** a ram instead. Ibrahim had passed Allah's test of faith. During the four-day festival of *Eid-e Qurban*, Muslims traditionally slaughter a ram as a symbol of Allah's **mercy**, and share the meat among family, friends, and the needy. They also visit their mosque to pray.

Eid-e Ghadeer

One year before his death, Muhammad led thousands of travelers on a pilgrimage to Mecca. On their way home, Muhammad is said to have stopped at an **oasis** called Ghadeer-e Khum. There, he announced that his cousin and son-in-law, Ali, would become the *imam*, or leader of Islam, after him. Shi'is celebrate *Eid-e Ghadeer* on the anniversary of Muhammad's announcement, the eighteenth day of the last month of the Muslim calendar, Dhu al-Hijjah. *Eid-e Ghadeer* is a proud day for Shi'is because their faith in the *imams* is based on this announcement. They celebrate by bringing gifts to *sayyids*, or people who claim to be Muhammad's descendants, and receive the *sayyids'* blessings in return.

Ashura

Black banners are hung over streets and public buildings on *Ashura*, a day of mourning for Imam Hussein. Imam Hussein was the third Shi'i *imam* and Muhammad's grandson. He was killed by rival Muslims in 680 A.D., near the city of Kerbala in Iraq. Hussein had refused to swear loyalty to the Muslim leader Yazid, whom he felt was a brutal leader.

On *Ashura*, groups of men dressed in black walk in processions through the streets of every city and village. These mourners beat themselves with chains as a reminder of Hussein's suffering.

(above) This fourteen-level cake was created to celebrate Imam Mahdi's birthday.

Imam Mahdi's birthday

On the eve of the birthday of the twelfth *imam*, Imam Mahdi, Shi'is gather by the thousands to praise him and Allah, and to enjoy fireworks. Shi'is believe that Imam Mahdi will return to Earth one day to save humankind. On this holiday, called *Moloud Imam Mahdi*, or the birthday of Imam Mahdi, Persian carpets are hung outside buildings, and colored lights and flags decorate the streets. Many of the decorations are green, the traditional color of Islam.

What day is it?
Three calendars are used in Iran. The Persian solar calendar, called *shamsi*, is Iran's official calendar. It begins on the first day of spring. Iranians also use the Muslim calendar to keep track of Muslim holidays, and the Gregorian calendar, which is used by western countries, for business with foreign nations.

On Ashura, groups of actors perform plays, called tazyeh, *that tell of the events that took place at Kerbala. In this scene, spectators watch the burning of Imam Hussein's tent.*

Nowrouz, the Persian New Year celebration, is a joyous festival that marks the beginning of spring. *Nowrouz* has its roots in the Zoroastrian belief that, in the last days of the year, the souls of the dead return to visit their families. To prepare for their ancestors' arrival and to welcome the new year, Iranians of all faiths clean, cook, organize their homes, and buy new clothes, if possible. Then, for thirteen days, they celebrate with parties, feasts, and gift-giving.

Haft-seen

As *Sa'at-e Tahvil*, the exact moment of the start of spring, approaches, Iranian families gather around a table set with the *haft-seen*. *Haft-seen*, or "seven *s*s," are seven items whose names begin with the "s" sound in the Persian language. These are *sabzeh*, which are lentil or wheat sprouts; a fruit called *senjed*, which comes from the lotus tree; an apple; wheat porridge; vinegar; crushed sumac berries; and garlic. Each food has a special meaning, such as sweetness, health, or wealth.

Items such as a goldfish in a bowl, to represent water; painted eggs, to represent fertility; candles, to represent fire; and a mirror, to represent the sky, are added to the haft-seen *as reminders of the items that early Persians used in celebrating* Nowrouz.

Chaharshanbeh Suri

In the days leading up to *Nowrouz*, performers dress up as the traditional mascot, Haji Firouz. Haji Firouz is believed to protect the souls of the dead. Wearing baggy red pants and blackening their faces with fireplace soot, performers dance and sing *Nowrouz* songs in the streets.

On the last Wednesday before *Nowrouz*, Iranians hold a celebration called *Chaharshanbeh Suri*, which means "Red Wednesday." The color red and fire traditionally represent life, and they have been used by Iranians to keep yellow, or evil, spirits away. On the night of *Chaharshanbeh Suri*, Iranians light fires and fireworks in village and city squares. Many young people jump over the fires, calling out, "Give me your red and take my yellow!" to cast out evil spirits and bring good luck.

(top) The festival of Chaharshanbeh Suri, *during which Iranians jump over fires, is believed to date back to 1725 B.C., when Zoroastrianism was Iran's main religion.*

Sa'at-e Tahvil!

According to tradition, a hard-boiled egg placed on a flat mirror will start to tremble and spin at the new year *Sa'at-e Tahvil*. Many Iranian children eagerly watch the egg while listening to a radio or television countdown to the new year. When the new year arrives, prayers are said, children receive gifts of money, and the family enjoys treats such as flatbread with white cheese and herbs, roasted nuts, and pastries.

Seezdeh Beh Dar!

The thirteenth day of *Nowrouz* is known as *Seezdeh Beh Dar*, which means "thirteen in the outdoors." It is considered good luck for Iranians to spend this day in the countryside. Families and friends bring the *sabzeh* from their *haft-seen* tables. The *sabzeh* are supposed to hold people's pain and suffering after being in their homes. At the end of the picnic day, everyone tosses the *sabzeh* into a river or stream to get rid of their pain and ensure a happy new year.

Two cousins play guitar during their family's Seezdeh Beh Dar *picnic in a park outside Tehran.*

Stews, rice, and more

Zoroastrian children enjoy sweets as part of a celebration at the temple in Chakchak.

Many Iranian holidays are celebrated with delicious feasts. For Iranians, green herbs are a symbol of the new life that comes with the spring season. For this reason, the traditional *Nowrouz* feast always includes rice seasoned with fresh herbs, usually served with fish. Another dish that is often prepared for festive occasions is *fesenjan*, a stew of chicken in walnut and pomegranate sauce.

Warm from the oven

Bread, or *naan*, is eaten daily in Iran. *Sangak* is a heavy bread, made of whole-wheat flour. It is baked in a brick oven over hot stones, which gives *sangak* its dimpled look. *Lavash* is a very flat, thin bread, similar to a tortilla, while *taftun* is crisp and thicker. Iranians begin their day with a breakfast of *naan*, along with cheese and tea, and sometimes eggs and fruit.

Lunch and dinner

Lunch is the main meal of the day in many Iranian homes, and often consists of thick soups and stews with rice. *Khoresht* is a stew made with chicken or beef, as well as vegetables, nuts, fruit, and other ingredients. It may be seasoned with dried limes, pomegranate juice, and spices such as cinnamon, turmeric, or saffron. Lamb and chicken kebabs are popular for lunch, as are *dolmeh*, grapevine leaves stuffed with meat, rice, and vegetables. Most evening meals are very light, and can include sandwiches or *kukus*, omelets made of potatoes or vegetables. Supper may also consist of warm bread with soup or yogurt, or pizza, which has become very popular in Iran.

Rice would be nice!

Rice is grown in the well-watered Caspian region of northern Iran. Iran's rice is long grained and has a hearty, nutty flavor. It is served as a main ingredient in many dishes or prepared as a side dish. Rice can be steamed or cooked slowly in a pot with butter or oil until a golden crust forms at the bottom. This dish is known as *tah dig*.

Many Iranians buy their bread, or naan, *fresh every day from the bakery, while others bake* naan *at home.*

Tea, anyone?

Pomegranate juice is a favorite Iranian drink, as is *doogh*, a refreshing yogurt drink. Iranians also enjoy strong coffee, but tea is the favorite hot beverage. Water for strong, black tea is boiled in an urn called a *samovar*, then the tea is left to steep in a teapot on top of the *samovar*. Iranians sweeten their tea by placing a lump of sugar between their front teeth, and straining the tea through the sugar. Most Iranians have a *samovar* at home, but tea is also served in teahouses across the country, where people gather to socialize. Cookies, cakes, and simple meals are also served in teahouses.

Dessert

Fruits, such as grapes, plums, dates, sour cherries, and cantaloupe, are a common way to end a perfect meal. Sweets have traditionally been reserved for afternoon tea, but are now being eaten after meals. *Baklava* is a delicious treat. It is made of paper-thin sheets of pastry, layered with a mixture of ground almonds and sugar, and baked in sweet syrup.

Teacups in Iran usually do not have handles, so people have to hold the cups very carefully near the rim so they do not burn their fingers.

Shir-berenj

Iranians enjoy a rice pudding called *shir-berenj*. It is cooked slowly with milk, sugar, and **rose water**, and is sometimes garnished with crushed nuts. You can make *shir-berenj* with an adult's help.

You will need:
2 cups (500 ml) water
1 cup (250 ml) rice
1/2 cup (125 ml) rose water, which is sold at some grocery stores, or vanilla extract
8 cups (2 L) milk
1 cup (250 ml) cream

What to do:
1. Heat water in a medium-sized pot until boiling.

2. Add rice, cover, and simmer over low heat for fifteen minutes.

3. Add milk and cook over medium heat, stirring occasionally, until most of the milk has evaporated and a thick sauce coats the rice.

4. Add rose water or vanilla extract and cook for one more minute.

5. Top with cream, and serve with sugar or jam.

Watermelon is traditionally eaten during the feast of Yalda, *on December 21.* Yalda *marks the longest night of the year. It was originally a Zoroastrian festival, but is now celebrated by most Iranians.*

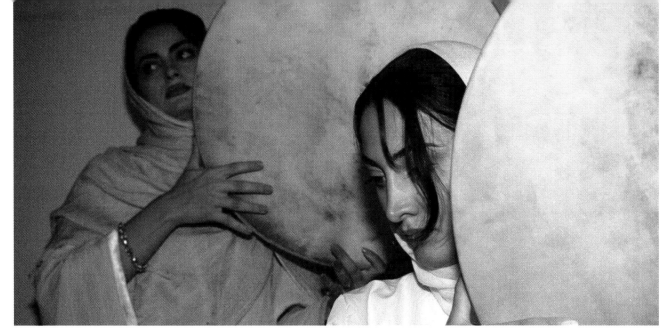

 # The music of Iran

Many musical instruments played in the West have roots in ancient Iranian instruments. The *nay*, or shepherd's reed, was a simple wooden tube with finger holes. It developed into several instruments, including one that looked like a flute and another that looked like Scottish bagpipes. The *kamancheh*, or Persian fiddle, was an early version of the violin and cello. It is still played today by classical and folk musicians in Iran.

(top) The daf, *an Iranian drum made of a wooden frame and animal skin, was traditionally used mainly in Sufi religious ceremonies.*

Classical Persian music

Iran's musical history stretches back to ancient times, but there have been periods since Islam was introduced to the country when all music, except for religious chants, was forbidden. Some versions of the *Hadith* describe music as an evil distraction from Allah. Even so, musicians continued to play classical Persian music secretly in their homes or at small private gatherings.

Today, classical Persian music is welcome in Iran. It is often performed by a small group, including a singer, two or three string players, and a drummer. The songs are based on the *radif*, a collection of melodies that were handed down from teachers to students. The soothing, hypnotic melodies of Persian music are meant to help listeners escape their thoughts and emotions and feel closer to Allah. Many followers of Sufism use classical Persian music in their ceremonies. Ancient Iranian poems are also sung to classical Persian music.

(left) In this painting from the early 1900s, Persian musicians play the sitar, *a stringed instrument with a pear-shaped body; the* kamancheh; *and the* santoor, *which has between 63 and 84 strings stretched across a flat wooden box.*

Popular music

Before the Islamic Revolution of 1979, many singers in Iran performed and recorded popular music. For nearly fifteen years after the revolution, only war hymns, traditional songs performed by men, and instrumental music were allowed to be played on government-owned radio stations and television channels. Many Iranian musicians left the country and continued to perform and record popular music in their new lands. Today, most western-produced pop music is still illegal, but many Iranians buy and sell it in secret. Iran now has its own popular music industry, which the government controls in order to ensure that the songs are acceptable by Muslim standards.

Musicians in Iran's national orchestra play instruments popular worldwide, such as the violin, as well as distinctively Iranian instruments, such as the kamancheh.

Iranian folk music

Iranian folk musicians play different types of songs for nearly every occasion, including weddings, **harvests**, and funerals. Each **ethnic group** has its own type of music, which is passed from one generation to the next. Although the songs are well known, folk music performers do a lot of improvising, making up new verses, changing lyrics, or creating interesting new melodies. The Kurds, a traditionally **nomadic** people from the western mountains, are famous for a type of folk music called *maqam*. *Maqam* is based on set patterns of notes, but the performer improvises the melody and rhythms. The festive songs of the Kurds are lively, and the audience often joins in by clapping and dancing.

The pop star Googoosh had an enormous following in Iran before the Islamic Revolution in 1979. She stayed in the country after the revolution, but was banned from singing. Her fans worldwide did not forget her, and 21 years later, Googoosh received permission to perform outside of Iran. She now has a renewed career and a new home in Toronto, Canada.

 # Iranian dance

In ancient Persia, professional dancers performed fire dances, sword dances, and dances performed while riding on horseback. They danced in the courts of shahs, or kings, at weddings, and during *Nowrouz* festivities. Today, all of Iran's peoples have developed local dances, which they perform during times of celebration.

Dancers from the province of Gilan, on the Caspian Sea coast, imitate the actions of the rice harvest in their traditional folk dances. Azari dance, from the northwestern province of Azerbaijan, features graceful, sweeping hand motions. In southwestern Iran, men from the Luri, Bakhtiari, and Qashqai ethnic groups perform *chub-bazi*, or stick-fighting dances.

(right) Public social dancing has been forbidden in Iran since the Islamic Revolution because traditional Muslim leaders believe it is immoral. Still, Iranian girls are taught Persian dance at home, and sometimes perform for friends and family at weddings and other private celebrations.

(top) An Iranian man dances to celebrate Seezdeh Beh Dar, *the last day of* Nowrouz.

Classical Persian dance

Two hundred years ago, in the courts of shahs, women performed what is known today as classical Persian dance. Persian dance involves expressive eyebrow, eye, and mouth movements that show emotions and tell a story. Dancers also use their hands in very expressive ways. Their feet step lightly and rhythmically, and they sometimes use finger cymbals to tap out the beat as they dance.

Made by hand

For more than 6,000 years, craftspeople in Iran have made pottery, bronze weapons, gold jewelry, and stone carvings. In the 500s B.C., sculptors carved an enormous image of the Persian king Darius I, as well as the story of his rise to the throne, into a cliffside known as Behistun Rock. Today, Iranian craftspeople create intricately engraved trays, dishes, and tea sets of copper, brass, and silver; fabrics with beautiful patterns; hand-embroidered scarfs; and jewelry made of turquoise, a gemstone found in Iran.

Calligraphy

Muslim leaders have not always approved of using human or animal images in religious artworks because the *Qur'an* tells Muslims that they must not worship **idols**. The *Hadith* also warns against portraying people and animals in art because Muslims believe that only Allah can create life.

Winged bulls decorate this cup made of gold, which is more than 2,700 years old.

Restrictions on art placed by Muslim leaders caused people to develop other art forms. Calligraphy is the art of decorative handwriting. Beautifully drawn Arabic or Persian script, along with leaves and stems arranged in repeating geometric patterns called arabesques, has decorated pottery, metal pitchers, and tiles in Iranian mosques and other buildings since the 600s A.D.

Many of Iran's books, especially the Qur'an and collections of poetry, have been handwritten in calligraphy.

Isfahan's Masjed-e Emam, which is also known as the Masjed-e Shah, is one of the most beautiful mosques in Iran. Its walls, floors, domes, and minarets are completely covered with bright blue ceramic tiles.

Tilework

Beautiful tilework has decorated buildings in Iran for at least 3,000 years, but the art of tilework developed greatly after the 1300s. Tiles are used to create mosaics or *haft rang* designs.

Mosaics are pictures made of colored stone or glazed ceramic tiles that are cemented together in an attractive pattern. With artworks made of *haft rang* tiles, or "seven colors" tiles, square, undecorated tiles are placed side by side into a large panel. Traditionally, an image or design was painted on the tiles with seven colors, but today, more than seven colors are used. Then, the uncemented tiles are removed from the panel and fired, or baked, individually in an oven called a kiln. After the tiles are fired, the design is cemented together.

Miniatures

Before the arrival of Islam, Iranian artists painted people and animals on pottery, **textiles**, and walls. Their paintings had vivid colors and often richly patterned backgrounds. When the Mongols came to power in Iran in the 1200s, they brought with them the Chinese technique of painting miniature, realistic scenes on paper. Iranian artists soon began painting in this style.

By the 1500s, works by Sufi poets had inspired artists to create even more detailed scenes with bolder colors. Iranian miniatures became famous all over the world. Iranian artists, such as Farah Ossouli, still create traditional miniature paintings that are shown in galleries across Iran and worldwide.

At first, miniatures decorated books, but over time they were also painted on single sheets of paper. Collectors of miniatures bound the paintings into albums.

23

Pottery

In the 800s, fine Chinese **porcelain** was popular in Iran. Iran's rulers encouraged the country's craftspeople to create pottery that had the same white, shiny look. The artisans developed a glaze that was whitened with powdered tin, and used it to paint their pots. Later, Iranian potters developed a technique called lusterware, in which items were first glazed and fired, then painted with metallic colors. A final firing gave the pieces a glossy, metallic finish. Today, Iranian potters create glazed **earthenware** pots, vases, and tiles in both traditional and modern styles.

Marquetry

Marquetry is the art of cutting thin pieces of wood, bone, shell, or metal into tiny shapes and gluing or cementing them into detailed patterns. Marquetry, or inlaid, designs decorate items, such as furniture, jewelry boxes, game boards, and wall hangings. The woods used by Iranian craftspeople for marquetry include walnut, pine, and cypress, and come in a variety of natural colors.

Painting and sculpture today

Farhad Moshiri (1963–) paints in Tehran, but displays his work in galleries throughout the world. One of his series of paintings depicts large, weathered ceramic jars like those sold in Iranian bazaars. Jamshid Moradian (1952–) is a sculptor whose works are inspired by Iran's thousands-year-old art history. Some of his sculptures are carved into dead tree trunks in Tehran's public spaces.

Many talented painters and sculptors work around Tehran, where there are several art galleries. The Tehran Museum of Contemporary Art displays a large collection of paintings and sculptures produced since the mid-1800s by Iranian and European artists. "Coffeehouse" art is an Iranian folk-painting style that originated in the 1500s. Artists paint religious and mythical scenes on the walls of coffeehouses and *zurkhaneh*, which are gyms where an Iranian martial art, *Varzesh-e Pahlavani*, is performed.

Contemporary Iranian artist Mostepha Darbaghi displays his paintings in his studio in Tehran.

Persian carpets are a central part of Iranian life and a world-famous symbol of Iranian culture. Carpets are laid on floors, spread out for picnics, used in religious ceremonies, and enjoyed as art. Iranians also kneel on carpets to pray.

Making carpets

Nomadic tribeswomen have traditionally woven Persian carpets, with each tribe specializing in particular patterns and colors. Classic Persian carpet designs include geometric, plant, or flower patterns. Carpets are now handwoven mostly by women in village and city workshops. Some are made by machine in Iranian factories.

Handwoven Persian carpets begin with spun, washed, dried, and dyed wool, which comes from sheep, goats, or camels. The most expensive carpets are made of silk. The carpet weaver stretches long threads across a wooden frame called a loom, and knots short pieces of wool or silk around the threads. The best carpets have at least 250 knots per square inch (40 knots per square centimeter).

A carpet's value

The value of a handmade Persian carpet depends on the quality of yarn used, the type of dye used to color the yarn, the detail of the design, and the number of knots per square inch. Natural dyes, which come from **minerals**, plants, and insects, are longer lasting and more soothing to the eye than artificial dyes. Antique Persian carpets, which have survived hundreds of years, have an especially high value. Carpets made in factories are less valuable because they often contain **synthetic** materials and are less unique-looking.

Carpetmaking today

Iran's young carpet designers continue to experiment with patterns and colors. Many base their work on traditional designs, but others create modern carpets inspired by the simple lines and bold colors of contemporary paintings. Afsaneh Modir Amani combines traditional and modern patterns to create designs for both factory-made and fine handwoven carpets.

(top) Weaving a Persian carpet by hand can take months or even years to finish, depending on the number of knots and the difficulty of the design.

 # Living languages

Iran's main language is Persian, which Iranians call Farsi. One half of Iranians speak Persian as a first language, but even Iranians whose mother tongue is Arabic, Armenian, Luri, Baluchi, or any other of Iran's 69 languages can also speak Persian.

Persian

When the Persians first came to Iran in the 1300s B.C., they brought along the Persian language. The ancient version of the language developed into the Persian spoken today, which includes many words borrowed from Arabic. Since the arrival of Islam in Iran, Persian has been written in a Perso-Arabic script, a form of the Arabic alphabet with four extra letters for Persian sounds.

(top) These girls speak Persian to one another in a park in Tehran. They also speak Persian at home and study Persian grammar and literature at school.

(above) Persian is written and read from right to left, not left to right as with English.

English	Persian
Hello.	*Salam.*
Goodbye.	*Khodafez.*
Welcome.	*Khosh amadid.*
How are you?	*Hal-e shoma khub e?* or *Hal-e shoma chetore?*
Please.	*Loftan.*
Thank you.	*Mersi.*
Yes.	*Bale.*
No.	*Na.*
What is your name?	*Esmetan chi st?*
Mother.	*Madar.*
Father.	*Pedar.*

Turkic languages

The mother tongue of more than twenty million Iranians is one of several Turkic languages. Northern and northeastern Iran are home to the Turkmen people, whose language is also called Turkmen. In Iran, Turkmen is only spoken, and not written. Speakers of Azari live mainly in the Azerbaijan region of northwestern Iran. They write their language using the Perso-Arabic alphabet. The Qashqai language, which is also written in Perso-Arabic, is spoken by Iran's Qashqai people, most of whom are herders in the southwestern province of Fars.

(right) The Bakhtiari people, who live in southwestern Iran, speak a dialect, or version, of Persian called Bakhtiari.

Kurdish

The Kurds of northwestern and northeastern Iran speak one of two dialects of Kurdish. More than three million Iranian Kurds speak the Kurdi dialect, while about 200,000 speak Kurmanji. Both dialects are related to Persian, and in Iran, are written using the Arabic script. Kurdish is a language rich with colorful sayings, such as, *"Rojek be ser bilindi, newek set sal be ser sori,"* which means, "One day with honor is better than one hundred with shame."

Arabic

During the 700s and 800s A.D., Arabic was Iran's official language. It was brought to the country by the conquering Muslim armies of present-day Saudi Arabia. Eventually, many of its words found their way into other Iranian languages, including Persian. Today, Arabic is the mother tongue of less than two percent of Iranians, yet religious Muslims read some Arabic every day, as it is the language of the *Qur'an*. Most Iranian Muslims who recite their prayers in Arabic cannot speak the language fluently.

The written word

The Zoroastrian holy book, the *Avesta*, contains Iran's first written poems. They are said to have been written down around 200 B.C. Thousands of years later, poetry is still an honored art form in Iran. Poets have been inspired by Persian **mythology**, the mysteries of Allah, and the beauty of the world around them.

The first classics

Poetry blossomed in Iran from the 800s to the 1100s. Abdollah Jafar ibn Mohammad Rudaki (858–941) composed **odes** to the king, and explored the themes of love, aging, and happiness in his work. Omar Khayyam (1048–1141) wrote the *Rubaiyat*, a book of **quatrains** that describe the pleasures of life.

Iranian masterpiece

Iran's history, legends, and lore, from mythical times through to the Arab conquest, were gathered and written as poetry by Hakim Abol-Ghasem Ferdowsi Toosi (940–1020). Ferdowsi spent 30 years perfecting his *Shahnameh*, or *Book of Kings*, which takes readers to mythical battlefields, shares words of everyday wisdom, and describes love stories. The *Shahnameh* is treasured not only for its wonderful stories, but also for its use of the early Persian language, which would otherwise be forgotten because it is no longer spoken.

Poetry in the 1200s and 1300s

Persian poetry reached its height in the 1200s and 1300s, with the work of Sufi poets. Sufis believe that the beauty of poetry, music, and dance comes from Allah, and that experiencing these art forms is a way of knowing Allah. Many Sufi poems describe the love between two people, but they may also be interpreted as describing the love between people and Allah.

Rumi, Sa'di, and Hafiz were among the best-known Sufi poets. Mevlana Jalal-e Din Mevlavi Rumi, who lived in the 1200s, wrote delicate poems of longing and joy, using simple words to share deep wisdom about life. One Rumi poem says, "For those who realize that everything is from God, everything is the same." Mohammad Shams al-Din Hafiz, who lived in the 1300s, wrote *ghazals* that explored love and religion. *Ghazals* are poems of six to fifteen **couplets**. Hafiz also wrote poems about history and about the people and places of Shiraz.

Collections of Hafiz's poems were often decorated with beautiful miniature paintings.

Mourners holding posters of Ahmad Shamlu lined the streets of Tehran after the poet's death.

Modern poetry

Much of the Iranian poetry written in the last century has been about the challenges of life in Iran. The first Iranian poet to tackle social issues, such as poverty and the unfair treatment of others, was Nima Yushij (1896–1959). Yushij used the ideas of night and day to describe difficult situations and hope for the future. Yushij inspired a whole new generation of writers, among them Ahmad Shamlu (1925–2000). Shamlu's works expressed a deep respect for his fellow human beings, and hope for a better future. Forough Farrokhzad (1935–1967) was the first Iranian woman to challenge traditional roles for women in her country through her poetry. Simin Behbahani (1927–) writes modern *ghazals* about events that shape the lives of the Iranian people.

Azar Nafisi, an Iranian who now lives in Washington, D.C., wrote Reading Lolita in Tehran *about her experiences teaching banned western literature to seven female students in her home.*

Fiction

Beginning around 1930, Iranians started to write and read more novels and short stories, in addition to poetry. Many of these were about the difficulties of living under the rule of the last two shahs. Some authors were put in prison because they spoke out against unfair rule. After the Islamic Revolution in 1979, writers were not allowed to create works that challenged Islam or criticized the policies of the government. Works celebrating Muslim values were encouraged. As a result of the **censorship**, many authors left Iran and continued to write from abroad.

Among Iran's most noted fiction writers are Simin Daneshvar, Moshen Makhmalbaf, and Moniru Ravanipur. Simin Daneshvar (1921–) writes short stories and novels that often challenge the traditional ways of Iranian society. Moshen Makhmalbaf (1957–) is a well known filmmaker, but he has also written novels and short stories that explore the issues of social freedoms and government control. Moniru Ravanipur is one of Iran's most promising young fiction authors. In her book of short stories, *Sangha-ye Shaytan,* or *Satan's Stones,* Ravanipur weaves tales about the lives of Iranian village women.

Tell me a story

In village teahouses across Iran, storytellers called *naqqals* recite famous Persian stories for spellbound crowds. *Naqqals* sometimes clap out the rhythm of the verses as their voices rise and fall with the stories' action. In this folktale from the *Shahnameh*, the fears of a powerful ruler nearly cost him the love of his son.

The Story of Zal

The tiny kingdom of Zabul buzzed with excitement. King Sam and his young queen were blessed with their first child, a boy. The baby's skin was as smooth as silk, his eyes were as black as night, and his lips were like a red bow, but his fine hair caused the biggest stir, for it glowed silvery white. No one had ever seen such a wondrous head of hair.

The people celebrated the new arrival, but King Sam was struck with fear. Could his son's unusual hair be a sign to him from the evil spirits? Was his kingdom in danger? The enemies of the great god Ahura Mazda were known to send warnings such as this. With a heavy heart, King Sam ordered that the baby be taken to the desert and left to die.

As evening neared, the great, magical bird Simurgh spotted the white-haired creature. In an instant, she swooped down and gathered him up for her babies to eat. As the baby lay in the birds' nest, high atop Mount Damavand, their hearts filled with love for him, and Simurgh decided to keep the baby as her own.

The years passed, and the baby grew into a brave, handsome boy. He spent his days running like the wind and leaping across the peaks of the Elburz Mountains, his long white hair flowing behind him.

In Zabul, King Sam was sick with grief. Over time, he had realized what a terrible mistake he had made, and his heart was broken. One night, as he lay waiting for sleep, his thoughts turned again to his child. "Ahura Mazda," he prayed, "I have committed such a cruel deed. Please guide me now so that I might do good."

That night, King Sam dreamed of a handsome boy leaping high over mountaintops. The boy had skin as smooth as silk, eyes as black as night, lips like a red bow, and pure white hair grown to his waist. When King Sam awoke, he felt sure that his son was alive.

King Sam went to the mountains and searched high and low. Simurgh spotted the king, and flew to find the boy. "That man is your father," she told him. "He has come to ask you for forgiveness." Then, Simurgh drew a sigh, and added, "It is time for you to go home."

Reunited with his son after so many years, King Sam fell to the ground to thank Ahura Mazda, and kissed the boy again and again. Simurgh placed the boy's hand in his father's, and bid them a good life. Before she flew away, she plucked one of her feathers and gave it to the boy. "Burn this feather if you are ever in trouble. Wherever you are, I will come to your side."

The boy, who was given the name Zal, grew up to be a mighty warrior, a fine horseman, and a leader beloved by all his people. No one was more proud of him, though, than his father, King Sam.

Glossary

altar A table or stand used for religious ceremonies

ancestor A person from whom another person or group is descended

atonement The act of asking for forgiveness for sins

censorship The act of deleting or changing artwork, films, books, and other publications that are considered offensive

couplet Two lines of poetry, one following the other, that often rhyme and have the same length

descendant A person who can trace his or her family roots to a certain family or group

earthenware Made from clay fired at low temperatures

empire A group of countries or territories under one ruler or government

ethnic group A group of people who share a common race, language, religion, and history

harvest The gathering of crops

Heaven The place where, according to some religions, the souls of good people go after they die

Hell The place where, according to some religions, the souls of people who have behaved badly on Earth go after they die

idol An image used as an object of worship

interpret To explain

mercy Compassion and kindness, especially shown to a person under one's power

mineral A naturally occurring, non-living substance obtained through mining

Muslim A person who follows the religion of Islam

mythology A collection of stories about a people's history, gods, goddesses, and heroes

nomadic Moving from season to season in search of food and water

oasis An area in a desert where plants grow because there is water

ode A formal poem, often written to praise someone

porcelain A hard, white ceramic

prophet A person believed to deliver messages from God

quatrain A verse or poem of four lines

republic A country led by an elected government rather than a king or queen

rose water A fragrant liquid made by boiling water with rose petals or rose oil

sacrifice To kill in a religious ceremony as an offering to God

savior A person who rescues another from harm or danger

shrine A place dedicated to a holy person

synthetic Made artificially, from chemicals

textile A fabric or cloth

trade The business of buying and selling products

Index

1 2 3 4 5 6 7 8 9 0 Printed in the U.S.A. 4 3 2 1 0 9 8 7 6 5